LEGENDS OF THE
NBA

Abbeville Kids
An Imprint of Abbeville Press
New York · London

Text by Kjartan Atli Kjartansson
Designer: Árni Torfason

For Abbeville Press
Project editors: Lauren Bucca and David Fabricant
Copy editor: Rodelinde Albrecht
Proofreader: Jennifer Dixon
Layout: Ada Rodriguez
Production manager: Louise Kurtz

PHOTOGRAPHY CREDITS

Getty Images: p. 35 (NBAE 1980/Ken Regan/NBAE), p. 53 (Tim DeFrisco/Allsport)

Megapixl: pp. 7, 13 and cover (right), 19, 23, 27, 31, 33 and cover (left), 41, 43, 45, 49, 51, 59, 61 (Wickedgood); pp. 9, 15 and cover (middle) (Brooklynboy321); pp. 17, 21, 37 (Cedul50); pp. 25, 62–63 (Rebelml); p. 29 (Swa1959); p. 39 (Spopho); p. 55 (Dgareri)

Shutterstock: pp. 1–2 (Eugene Onischenko); pp. 3–4 (The Len)

Wikimedia Commons: p. 11 (unknown author), p. 47 (Vernon J. Biever); p. 57 (Barry Bregman)

Please note: This book has not been authorized by the NBA.

First edition
10 9 8 7 6 5 4 3

Library of Congress Cataloging-in-Publication Data

Names: Kjartan Atli Kjartansson, 1984- author.
Title: Legends of the NBA / Kjartan Atli Kjartansson.
Description: First edition. | New York, N.Y.: Abbeville Kids, an imprint
  of Abbeville Press, 2022. | Series: Basketball legends | Audience: Ages
  9–12 years | Audience: Grades 4-6 | Summary: "Illustrated profiles of
  twenty-eight basketball legends"— Provided by publisher.
Identifiers: LCCN 2022035885 | ISBN 9780789214430 (hardcover)
Subjects: LCSH: Basketball players—United States—Biography—Juvenile literature.
Classification: LCC GV884.A1 K528 2022 | DDC 796.323092/2
  [B]—dc23/eng/20220812
LC record available at https://lccn.loc.gov/2022035885

For bulk and premium sales and for text adoption procedures, write to Customer Service Manager, Abbeville Press, 655 Third Avenue, New York, NY 10017, or call 1-800-ARTBOOK.

Visit Abbeville Kids online at www.abbeville family.com.

CONTENTS

ABDUL-JABBAR

When we think of smart basketball players, Kareem Abdul-Jabbar immediately comes to mind. He won titles at all levels of basketball, scored almost at will, and inspired his teammates.

Abdul-Jabbar won six NBA championships, first with the Milwaukee Bucks and later with the Los Angeles Lakers. When his NBA career ended after 20 seasons, he was the highest-scoring player, the top rebounder, and the top shot-blocker in the history of the league.

This amazing player, who had such great athletic ability and mental strength, grew up in Harlem and fell in love with basketball early on. He was born Lewis (Lew) Alcindor but adopted the name Kareem Abdul-Jabbar at age 24, when he converted to Islam.

At 7'2", he was taller than any of his peers. He is said to have dunked for the first time when he was in the eighth grade, much to the delight of those present. When he got to high school, his career took off. He led the Power Memorial Academy to three city titles, and the team lost only one game with him on the board. The young center's success attracted attention on a national level, and the legendary UCLA coach John Wooden offered him a scholarship.

Abdul-Jabbar joined the UCLA freshman team, because in those days first-year students weren't allowed to play for NCAA varsity teams. The first game of the year was between the freshman team and the varsity team. Nobody thought the freshmen would have much of a chance—they had never beaten the varsity team before, and the varsity team had just won two NCAA championships in a row.

But Abdul-Jabbar and his teammates defied expectations. The freshman team won the game 75–60 in front of more than 12,000 spectators. Abdul-Jabbar scored 31 points and took 20 rebounds.

The next year, he finally got to play for the varsity team. In his first varsity game, he scored 56 points, breaking the UCLA record. That season, the team won 30 games and lost none, taking the NCAA title. And their stellar center became known as the "New Superstar." Abdul-Jabbar was so dominant that the NCAA board decided to ban dunking in an attempt to diminish his superiority. (The ban lasted for more than a decade.)

Abdul-Jabbar played three seasons for UCLA's varsity team, and they were NCAA champions all three years. They won 88 games during this time and lost only 2. One loss was against the University of Houston, where Abdul-Jabbar sustained an eye injury, and the other was against their rival USC. In that game, the USC coach took advantage of the fact that there was no shot clock in the NCAA at the time, and had his team do everything they could to stall the game. Abdul-Jabbar took just four shots in that game and scored 10 points.

POSITION: CENTER
BORN: APRIL 16, 1947
HEIGHT: 7 FT 2 IN
TEAMS: MILWAUKEE BUCKS (1969–75), LOS ANGELES LAKERS (1975–89)

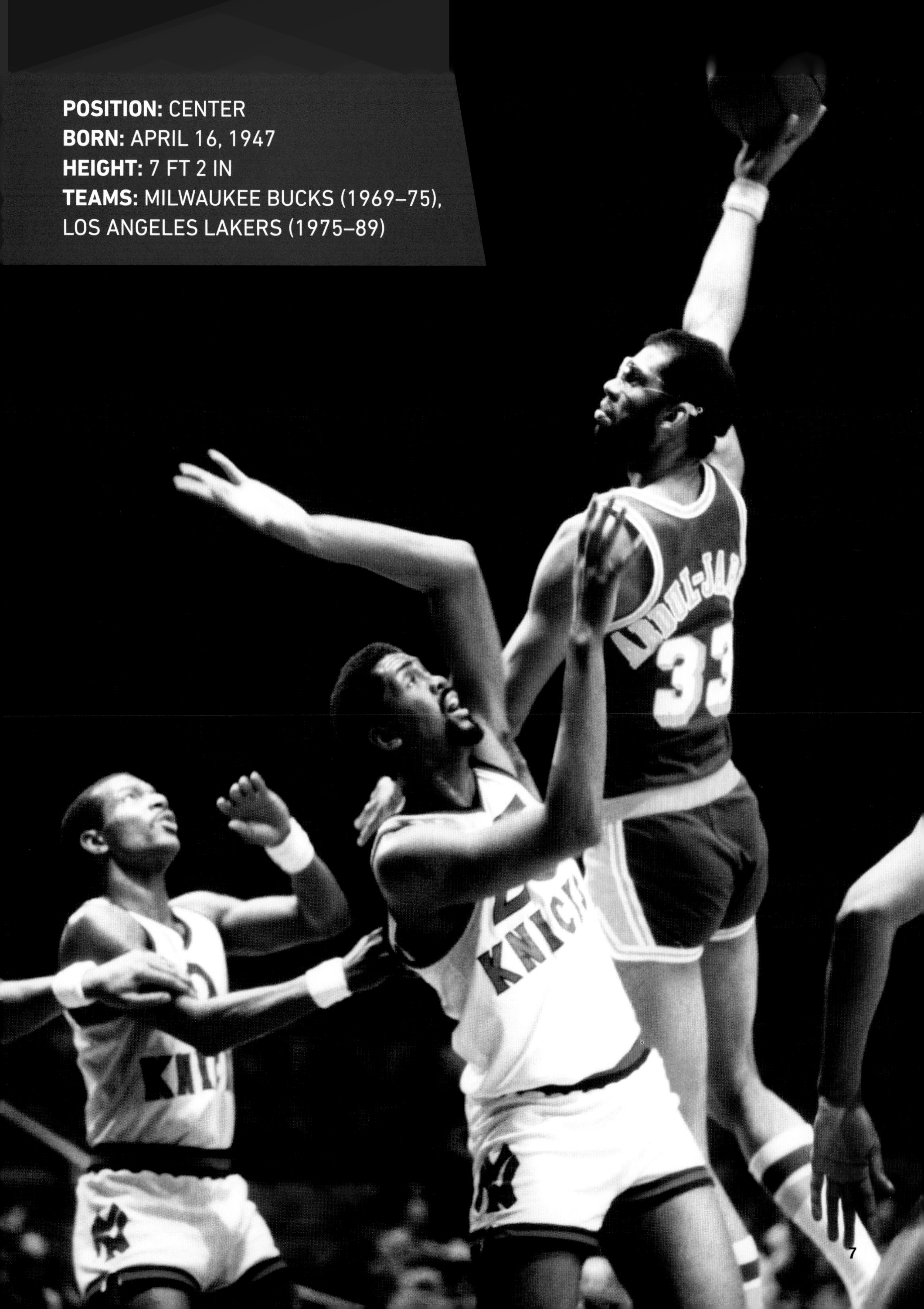

BARKLEY

Nowadays, Charles Barkley is best known as an outspoken basketball analyst on TNT, but he was just as entertaining to watch as a basketball player.

Born in Leeds, Alabama, Barkley was a promising youth player. He was raised by his mother and grandmother, and is said to have inherited his well-known sense of humor from his grandmother.

He decided to go to Auburn University, where he played alongside Chuck Person, who also had a good NBA career. Barkley graduated in 1984 and hoped to go to the Olympics with the US national team that year. In those days, professionals were not allowed to play on the national team, so the best college players were often recruited instead. It turned out that Barkley was not chosen for the Olympics, but he used this setback as motivation to come into the NBA as a force to be reckoned with.

He was selected fifth in the draft that year by a strong Philadelphia 76ers team. Some people doubted that Barkley could become an effective NBA player, because in those days he was considered too short, at 6'6", to be a power forward. But he would soon disprove that theory.

The Sixers had players like Moses Malone, Maurice Cheeks, Andrew Toney, and the legendary Julius Erving ("Dr. J."). The team had won the championship two years before Barkley entered the league, and it would have been a challenge for any newcomer to stand out on such a strong squad. But Barkley averaged 14 points per game in his rookie year. Still, the team only made it to the Eastern Conference Finals that season, which was no doubt a disappointment. The Sixers board

then made some controversial decisions, which included transferring Moses Malone to the Washington Bullets. Philadelphia's title hopes faded, and Barkley seemed more irritated with each passing year.

Despite the difficult circumstances at the Sixers, Barkley managed to fulfill his Olympic dreams in 1992, when he was chosen for the US national team that played at the games in Barcelona. This was the first Olympics in which NBA players were allowed to compete, and the US team boasted such an array of talent that it was nicknamed the "Dream Team." Barkley attracted a lot of attention at the games, where he was the Dream Team's highest-scoring player. He gave entertaining interviews, too. After the Olympics many companies hired him to appear in advertisements.

After the Olympics, Barkley was traded to the Phoenix Suns, where he was part of a strong team that reached the finals against the Chicago Bulls. It was a memorable duel in which Barkley faced off against his Dream Team teammates Michael Jordan and Scottie Pippen. The Bulls ended up winning the championship, but Barkley was named that season's MVP.

Despite repeated attempts, Barkley failed to win an NBA championship before retiring from basketball. However, Sir Charles, as he was called, is considered one of the best power forwards in the history of the NBA. He was on the All-NBA First Team five times and the All-NBA Second Team five times. He played in 11 All-Star Games and finished with an average of 22 points, 12 rebounds, and four assists per game over his career.

POSITION: POWER FORWARD
BORN: FEBRUARY 20, 1963
HEIGHT: 6 FT 6 IN
TEAMS: PHILADELPHIA 76ERS (1984–92), PHOENIX SUNS (1992–96),
HOUSTON ROCKETS (1996–2000)

BAYLOR

Even though he spent his entire career with the same team, Elgin Baylor played at two home arenas almost 2,000 miles apart. He joined the Lakers in 1958, when they were still in Minneapolis, and in 1960 he moved with them from the cold Midwest to the sunshine of Los Angeles, where he became a legend. As a pioneer of the slam dunk, Baylor is considered the first aerial master of the NBA. But he was also a great shooter and could score almost at will.

Baylor was born in Washington, DC, and went to high school there. Because the college scouts did not recruit from Black high schools at that time, he began his college career at a small school, the College of Idaho. After one year there, Baylor transferred to Seattle University, where he managed to lead the school to the NCAA finals in his junior year. At the end of that season, he was drafted by the Minneapolis Lakers.

The Lakers were a fading force at the time. The first NBA superstar, George Mikan, had retired from the team in 1954, four years before Baylor entered the league. The Lakers were known for playing a slow-paced brand of basketball that brought limited results—the season before Baylor's arrival, they were last in the league. But in his first season, Baylor led this struggling team all the way to the finals against Boston Celtics, only to lose this final duel. He was crowned Rookie of the Year.

The Lakers' owner later said that if he had not been able to negotiate with Baylor, the franchise would have gone bankrupt. With Baylor on board, the Lakers once again became a marketable commodity, and the decision was made to relocate the team to the booming market of Los Angeles.

In Los Angeles, Baylor's career reached new heights, and he gained an important new teammate: the Lakers drafted the young Jerry West in 1960, the year of their move. West and Baylor would go on to become one of the greatest duos in NBA history. Baylor's performance in the 1961–62 season was particularly remarkable, because he had been called up to active military service in Fort Lewis, Washington. He couldn't train with the team and was only able to play with them on the weekends. But he still averaged 38.3 points per game!

In 1968, Wilt Chamberlain joined Baylor and West on the Lakers. The team was dominant in the regular season but never managed to win an NBA title. Baylor reached the NBA finals a total of eight times without taking the championship.

The 1971–72 season turned out to be Baylor's last. He had torn his Achilles tendon in the previous season and had not regained his strength. After only nine games, he decided to stop playing, because he felt he could not perform at the highest level anymore. That season, however, turned out to be the best in the history of the Lakers: the team set a record by winning 33 games in a row and went on to win the championship. The Lakers board awarded Baylor a championship ring even though he had retired at the start of the season.

POSITION: SMALL FORWARD
BORN: SEPTEMBER 16, 1934
DIED: MARCH 22, 2021
HEIGHT: 6 FT 5 IN
TEAM: MINNEAPOLIS/LOS ANGELES LAKERS (1958–71)

BIRD

Larry Bird grew up in the small town of French Lick, Indiana, which earned him the nickname "the Hick from French Lick." But his other nickname is "Larry Legend," because he is truly one of the greatest players of all time. Bird joined the Boston Celtics in 1979 and stayed with them his entire career, taking the team to five NBA finals and three NBA championships. Bird and his teammates in green changed the face of the sport along with their archrivals, the Los Angeles Lakers.

In March 1985, Bird became the first Celtics player to score 60 points in a game, in a matchup with the Atlanta Hawks. This broke the previous record of 56 points that Bird's teammate, the great Kevin McHale, had set just nine days before.

But Bird's performance in that game against the Hawks was memorable for more than just his total score. At one point Bird asked the Hawks, "The trainer's lap, who wants it?"—meaning that he intended to throw a deep three-pointer from where the Hawks' trainer was sitting at the edge of the court. Doc Rivers, who played for Hawks at the time, recalled, "I think it was Rickey Brown who tried to stop Bird, who took a rainbow shot high into the air that went straight into the hoop. Rickey ran into Bird and stumbled, so he fell right into the trainer's lap, just as Bird had said would happen." Rivers says it was, of course, a coincidence and an accident.

Many legends swirl around that game. Some say that Bird went into it in less than peak con-dition, because he had run in a five-mile charity race two days earlier. Others have even claimed that he was hungover from a party the night before—which Bird has denied.

But one thing is clear: Bird's performance was amazing. So amazing, in fact, that the Hawks cheered some of the baskets that Bird scored.

The best Celtics team Bird played with—and certainly one of the best basketball teams of all time—was the championship-winning team of 1986. Their passing interplay was almost poetic, and no individual player was more important than the team. Each player in the starting line-up averaged 10 points or more, and backing them up on the bench was Bill Walton, who was once named the league's Most Valuable Player. This amazing team lost only three games in the playoffs.

The most memorable game of that year's playoffs was the second one in the Celtics' series against the Chicago Bulls. The standout on the court was a young player for the Bulls who scored 63 points: Michael Jordan. Despite Jordan's unstoppable performance, the game went into overtime twice, and Boston eventually won 135–131.

Larry Bird is the only forward in NBA history to receive the MVP Award three consecutive times. He was also Rookie of the Year, an All-Star Game MVP, a two-time Finals MVP, and a member of the famous Olympic Dream Team in 1992.

POSITIONS: SMALL/POWER FORWARD
BORN: DECEMBER 7, 1956
HEIGHT: 6 FT 9 IN
TEAM: BOSTON CELTICS (1979–92)

BRYANT

Nicknamed "Black Mamba," Kobe Bryant spent his entire career with the Los Angeles Lakers, bringing them to victory time and time again. He won five NBA championships and was an 18-time All-Star (the second-highest total in NBA history), a 15-time member of the All-NBA Team, an NBA MVP, and a two-time NBA Finals MVP.

Basketball was in Bryant's blood. His father, Joe Bryant, was an NBA player and later a coach. Inspired by his father, Bryant became passionate about the game, and dreamed of one day joining his favorite team, the Lakers. He went to Lower Merion High School in Ardmore, Pennsylvania, where he led the basketball team to a state championship and attracted national attention. After high school, he knew only one thing was next, and it wasn't college—it was the NBA.

Bryant was selected by the Charlotte Hornets as the thirteenth pick in the 1996 draft, but they traded him to the Lakers as part of a deal that had been arranged previously. He made the All-Star team in just his second season, and with his teammate—and rival—Shaquille O'Neal, helped lead the team to three NBA championships. After O'Neal was traded to the Miami Heat in 2004, Bryant cemented his status as the Lakers' greatest player.

He made his mark in history on January 22, 2006, when he scored 81 points in a game against the Toronto Raptors. This remains the second-highest number of points scored in a single game, behind only Wilt Chamberlain's famous 100-point game in 1962. However, some say that Bryant's record is just as impressive, since there were more scoring opportunities in Chamberlain's day.

Kobe Bryant was a role model for many of the current stars in the NBA. He was one of the hardest-working players in the world and was always ready to go the extra mile to improve. When he played for the US national team—winning gold medals in the 2008 and 2012 Olympics—his teammates were fascinated by his work ethic. Kevin Durant recalls a time at the national team training camp when "we had the day off, but they said we could get some shots up if we wanted." So Durant decided to take the bus to the training court with Jeff Green, his teammate on the Oklahoma City Thunder. "Kobe was the only guy on the bus, and that spoke volumes to me—he's the best player in the game, yet he's always willing to come work on his game."

It is hard to beat Bryant's record. He is still the leading scorer in Lakers history, he was the first guard to play 20 seasons in the NBA, and he is tied with Bob Pettit for the most All-Star Game MVP Awards in NBA history. No doubt Bryant would still be making his mark on the world if he were here today—however, he tragically died in a helicopter crash in 2020, along with his daughter Gianna. His legacy has been honored in many ways by his countless fans as well as the NBA. After his death, the All-Star Game MVP trophy was renamed the Kobe Bryant MVP Award.

POSITION: SHOOTING GUARD
BORN: AUGUST 23, 1978
DIED: JANUARY 26, 2020
HEIGHT: 6 FT 6 IN
TEAM: LOS ANGELES LAKERS (1996–2016)

When Vince Carter was a student at Mainland High School in Daytona Beach, Florida, he was so athletic that he probably could have received a college scholarship in three different sports. He played quarterback on the school's football team until he broke his wrist, at which point he switched to volleyball and quickly became a standout. Once his wrist recovered, though, he decided to focus on basketball.

There he also attracted the attention he deserved. He led Mainland to its first state title in 56 years and was a McDonald's All-American in 1995. He was scouted by the college powerhouses. (As further evidence of his many talents, he was also offered a saxophone scholarship by Bethune-Cookman University.) Carter ended up going to the University of North Carolina, where he was part of a strong team that won two ACC titles and went to the Final Four twice. He spent three years in college and finished with 15.6 points per game over his college career.

Carter entered the league in 1998. He was chosen fifth in the first round of the draft by the Golden State Warriors, who traded him to the Toronto Raptors. Carter was in fact the first star to play for the franchise, which had been founded in 1995. He was instrumental in establishing basketball in Toronto, even though his parting with the Raptors was not the best.

In the '90s, basketball fans would tune into *NBA Action* to see the countdown of the top 10 plays of the week. Carter's incredible shots often appeared in these highlight reels. In his third year with the Raptors, he scored an average of 27.6 points, had a 41 percent three-point percentage, and averaged 5.5 rebounds and 3.9 assists.

Carter lasted longer than any other player of his generation in the league. He was 43 years old when he retired and is the only player in NBA history to have played in four different decades. Although Carter never won an NBA championship and only reached the Conference Finals once, he is an NBA icon. He was Dunk Champion in 2000, with one of the best performances in the history of the competition. He also knew how to score points: when he retired, he was one of the top 20 scorers in NBA history. And, with the incredible leaping ability that earned him the nickname "Vinsanity," he was always one of the most entertaining players to watch.

POSITIONS: SHOOTING GUARD/SMALL FORWARD
BORN: JANUARY 26, 1977
HEIGHT: 6 FT 6 IN
TEAMS: TORONTO RAPTORS (1998–2004), NEW JERSEY NETS (2004–9), ORLANDO MAGIC (2009–10), PHOENIX SUNS (2010–11), DALLAS MAVERICKS (2011–14), MEMPHIS GRIZZLIES (2014–17), SACRAMENTO KINGS (2017–18), ATLANTA HAWKS (2018–20)

CARTER

CHAMBERLAIN

Few players have dominated the NBA like Wilt Chamberlain. This 7'1" center was already famous by the time he entered the league. In the 1950s, players were not allowed to enter the NBA draft until four years after they had graduated high school. Because Chamberlain left the University of Kansas after his junior year, he had to wait a year before he could enter the NBA. So, in the meantime, he joined the Harlem Globetrotters. As a sign of Chamberlain's popularity, his contract with the Globetrotters was on a par with what many NBA stars were being paid. He traveled the world with the Globetrotters, even going to the Soviet Union.

In 1959, Chamberlain joined the Philadelphia Warriors (later the Golden State Warriors). He was absolutely unstoppable in his rookie year. In one game, he scored 58 points and grabbed 42 rebounds, setting an NBA record. In fact, Chamberlain broke eight separate NBA records in his first year in the league and was named Rookie of the Year and All-Star Game MVP.

But Chamberlain did not always enjoy playing and hinted that he intended to quit the league because he was always marked tightly by his opponents and the fouls got worse by the day. He was also a target of spectators and often said, "Nobody roots for Goliath." To keep him from leaving, the Warriors' board offered him a substantial amount of money. The year before, he had signed the biggest rookie contract in NBA history, but now his salary was doubled.

Chamberlain continued to dominate the NBA. But in his third year, he did something that will probably never be repeated: he scored 100 points in a single game. There was little anticipation for the game, a matchup between the War-

riors and the New York Knicks at the Hershey Sports Arena in Pennsylvania. There were five games left in the regular season; the Warriors were in second place in the Eastern Conference, and the Knicks were at the bottom.

The game got off to a brisk start. After just a few minutes, the score was 19–3 to the Warriors, with Chamberlain already on 13 points. The Knicks were without their starting center, so two understudies had to take turns marking Chamberlain. They were both considerably smaller than him and made little headway.

In the third quarter, Chamberlain really took off. The Knicks tried to double-, triple-, or even quadruple-team him, but he always managed to score or get on the free-throw line. He scored a total of 28 points in the quarter and was on 69 points when the fourth quarter started. The Knicks, who were losing by a wide margin, tried their best to prevent Chamberlain from scoring 100 points. The Warriors then started fouling the Knicks players in turn, in order to stop the clock and send them to the free-throw line. This created more opportunities for the Warriors to take back the ball and get it to Chamberlain.

With just over two minutes left, Chamberlain had scored 94 points. He then deftly turned to shoot and scored his 96th point. With 1:19 left, he dunked the ball to reach 98 points. In the last minute, Chamberlain missed a few shots around the basket, but his teammates caught the ball and passed it back to him. With 46 seconds left, he sunk the ball in to reach 100 points. The crowd went wild and rushed onto the court to congratulate Chamberlain.

POSITION: CENTER
BORN: AUGUST 21, 1936
DIED: OCTOBER 12, 1999
HEIGHT: 7 FT 1 IN
TEAMS: PHILADELPHIA/SAN FRANCISCO WARRIORS (1959–65),
PHILADELPHIA 76ERS (1965–68), LOS ANGELES LAKERS (1968–73)

DUNCAN

If Tim Duncan had stayed in his original sport, basketball fans would have missed out on one of the greatest players in history. Duncan, who was born and raised in Saint Croix in the US Virgin Islands, started out as a swimmer. As a boy, he swam every day with the goal of reaching the Olympics, as his older sister Tricia did in 1988.

But when Duncan was 13, Hurricane Hugo swept across the US Virgin Islands and caused widespread devastation. One of the buildings destroyed by the hurricane contained the only Olympic-size swimming pool in the territory. Duncan, who had been aiming for the 1992 Olympics, was left without a place to practice his sport.

On the advice of his family and friends, Duncan then decided to try his hand at basketball. Despite his relatively late start, he quickly attracted the attention of coaches for top college teams. He chose to go to Wake Forest after connecting with coach Dave Odom.

In the late '90s, players were entering the NBA at an increasingly young age. In previous years, most players had chosen to develop their game in college basketball before joining the league. But new stars like Kevin Garnett, Kobe Bryant, and Tracy McGrady were now being drafted straight out of high school.

Because Duncan had only started playing in the ninth grade, he decided to do things the old-fashioned way and spend four years in college working on his game. He got off to a slow start with Wake Forest and did not score any points in his first game for the team. But then he began to grow, both physically and mentally, and became an unstoppable force. He led his team

deep into the finals of the ACC conference every year and collected many individual accolades: he was named NABC Defender of the Year three times, ACC Player of the Year two times, and Consensus National College Player of the Year in 1997. In 1996, he led the ACC in points, rebounds, field goal percentage, *and* blocked shots—a record that remains undefeated.

NBA executives awaited Duncan with great anticipation. It has even been said that some of the teams not headed to the finals might have tanked their records in order to increase their chances of getting the number one draft pick. In any event, the first pick went to the San Antonio Spurs, and they chose Duncan.

At the Spurs, Duncan had only one coach, Gregg Popovich, who took over the year before Duncan joined the league. The two were the perfect combo. Popovich led the team off the court and knew he could trust the calm and intelligent Duncan to lead them on the court.

Despite being in a relatively small market, the Spurs put together a star-studded team, thanks to their great scouting system. The Spurs got both Tony Parker and Manu Ginóbili as relatively late draft picks, Parker at the end of the first round and Ginóbili at the end of the second round, making him one of the most undervalued draft picks of all time. Together, Duncan, Parker, and Ginóbili were the "Big Three" who made the Spurs a dominant force from 2002 to 2016.

Duncan won a total of five titles in the NBA, was named MVP twice, and was chosen 10 times for the All-NBA First Team. He is unarguably one of the all-time greats.

POSITIONS: POWER FORWARD/CENTER
BORN: APRIL 25, 1976
HEIGHT: 6 FT 11 IN
TEAM: SAN ANTONIO SPURS (1997–2016)

ERVING

Julius Erving was born and raised on Long Island and went to Roosevelt High School, where a friend gave him a nickname that stuck: "Dr. J." One sportswriter said that Erving was the Thomas Edison of basketball, because every night he invented some new move that other players wanted to emulate. Dr. J's game was known for its smooth elegance; in many ways he resembled an artist as much as an athlete.

In 1968, Erving went to the University of Massachusetts at Amherst, where he excelled, scoring an average of more than 20 points per game. After two years at UMass, Erving was impatient to go pro. At the time, the NBA would not draft players until they were at least four years out of high school. But in the now-defunct ABA (American Basketball Association), a league that competed with the NBA, players could apply for a "hardship exemption" that allowed them to join at a younger age.

That is how Erving ended up with the Virginia Squires of the ABA. He flourished as a player, but the Squires, like many ABA teams, were struggling financially. After two more years, he was finally eligible for the NBA draft, and he was selected by the Milwaukee Bucks.

But there was a problem. Shortly before the NBA draft, Erving discovered that his agent was on the Squires' payroll and had advised him to sign a contract that was below market value. In the ensuing dispute, Erving signed a contract with the Atlanta Hawks of the NBA. The result was that the Bucks, the Hawks, and the Squires all claimed Erving as their player, and the matter had to be settled in court. The judge sent Erving back to the Squires, and he had an amazing season with them, averaging 32 points per game.

The Squires were running low on cash, however, so they decided to trade their greatest asset, Erving, to another ABA team, the New York Nets. Erving won two ABA titles with the Nets, the second in 1976. That same year marked the end of the ABA, and four ABA teams, including the Nets, joined the NBA. The Nets undoubtedly had the biggest star—everyone was looking forward to seeing Dr. J in the NBA. But not everybody was happy with the merger: the New York Knicks sued the New York Nets for almost $5 million for invading the Knicks' NBA territory.

Even though the Nets succeeded in joining the NBA, they were in a shaky financial situation, and once again Dr. J. was traded for cash: he went to the Philadelphia 76ers in a deal worth $6 million. It took Erving several years to win a title with the Sixers, but his opportunity finally came in 1983. Dr. J was the star of that amazing championship team, along with Moses Malone. Maurice Cheeks, the point guard, was selfless and a great defender, and Bobby Jones and Andrew Toney were also part of a strong core.

Erving's career began at a strange time in professional basketball, and he encountered more obstacles than most superstars of his caliber. Still, there are few others who can say that they were the champion and MVP of two separate leagues.

POSITION: SMALL FORWARD
BORN: FEBRUARY 22, 1950
HEIGHT: 6 FT 7 IN
TEAMS: VIRGINIA SQUIRES (1971–73),
NEW YORK NETS (1973–76),
PHILADELPHIA 76ERS (1976–87)

Kevin Garnett was a high-school standout. In his senior year, he led Farragut Career Academy in Chicago to a 28–2 record and was named National High School Player of the Year by *USA Today*. He averaged 25.2 points, 17.9 rebounds, 6.7 assists, and 6.5 saves per game. All the best college programs in the country were after him, but Garnett decided to go straight to the NBA and was chosen by the Minnesota Timberwolves with the fifth pick in the 1995 draft. He was the first player since 1975 to be drafted straight from high school.

It took Garnett some time to adjust to the NBA—he had to put in a lot of effort because of how light he was. But ultimately he pulled off quite a respectable performance in his first year and was selected for the All-Rookie Second Team.

In the following seasons, Garnett developed quickly. He delivered great statistics and was a great leader as well: suddenly the Timberwolves were winning 40 to 50 games per season, rather than 20 to 30. In his fourth year in the league, Garnett averaged more than 20 points and 10 rebounds per game for the first time, a standard he would maintain for the next nine years. He also had around five assists, two blocked shots, and one stolen ball per game.

In 2007, Garnett was traded to the Boston Celtics, where he formed a strong partnership with Paul Pierce and Ray Allen. The Celtics won the championship in 2008, ending Boston's 22-year wait for a title. It didn't hurt that their opponents were their archrivals, the Lakers. Garnett was the first player in Celtics history to be named NBA Defender of the Year.

The Celtics were also very strong the following year, but Garnett was injured in February and missed the rest of the season. Then, in Garnett's third year with the Celtics, the team returned to the finals but lost to the Lakers in the seventh game. After that the Celtics failed to make it to the finals with the same lineup, and chief executive Danny Ainge decided to trade Garnett and Pierce to the Brooklyn Nets and start a new rebuild in 2013. At the Nets, Garnett and Pierce failed to live up to high expectations, and Garnett returned to the Timberwolves in 2015 to end his NBA career where it started.

Garnett was the third NBA player ever to score more than 25,000 points, take more than 14,000 rebounds, and give more than 5,000 assists. In his 21 years in the NBA, he was on the All-Defensive First Team nine times and was league Rebounding Champion four times. However, he made his greatest mark on the history of the Minnesota Timberwolves. In fact, the 2021–22 season was only the second in the history of the franchise in which they achieved more than a .500 record without Kevin Garnett, aka "the Big Ticket."

POSITION: POWER FORWARD
BORN: MAY 19, 1976
HEIGHT: 6 FT 11 IN
TEAMS: MINNESOTA TIMBERWOLVES (1995–2007), BOSTON CELTICS (2007–13), BROOKLYN NETS (2013–15), MINNESOTA TIMBERWOLVES (2015–16)

GARNETT

HAVLICEK

"Havlicek stole the ball!" is one of the most iconic radio calls in basketball history. Johnny Most, the voice of the Celtics for nearly four decades, was giving a play-by-play of the seventh game between the Boston Celtics and the Philadelphia 76ers at the Eastern Conference Finals in 1965. There were five seconds to go, and the Sixers needed just one basket to win the game. Sixers guard Hal Greer lobbed the ball toward his teammate Chet Walker—and that's when John Havlicek jumped in and deflected the pass with his right hand, saving the win for the Celtics.

Havlicek grew up in Martins Ferry, Ohio, and showed himself to be a versatile athlete early on. He could have gone to college on a football scholarship, but instead he chose to play basketball for Ohio State, where he was part of a very strong team that won the NCAA championship in 1960. His roommate was Jerry Lucas, who would become a seven-time NBA All-Star. Another teammate was Bobby Knight, who would go on to a legendary coaching career at Indiana University.

In 1962, Havlicek was drafted by the Boston Celtics as the seventh overall pick. But, in the same year, he was also chosen by the Cleveland Browns in the NFL draft, even though he had not played football since high school. Dissatisfied with the contract the Celtics offered him, Havlicek reported to the Browns' training camp as a wide receiver. It was only after he was cut from the Browns that he decided to join the Celtics after all.

At the Celtics, Havlicek once again found himself among legends. Center Bill Russell was an electrifying on-court leader, and the team's coach, Red Auerbach, was one of the most brilliant in basketball history. Red, as he was always called, developed a new role for Havlicek, that of the "sixth man." When the opponent's starting lineup began to get tired, Havlicek was brought off the bench and often managed to strengthen the Celtics' play. Even if he wasn't one of the starting five, he usually played a lot of minutes.

The Celtics won the NBA championship in each of Havlicek's first four seasons in the league, and they would win it four more times during his career. When he retired, Havlicek had played the most games in NBA history and the most games in the playoffs. He was the third highest-scoring player in NBA history and the Celtics' highest-scoring player, a record that still stands. Havlicek was also known for his defensive play, appearing five times on the All-Defense First Team and three times on the Second Team.

Havlicek, or "Hondo" as he was often called, was always ready to come off the bench and get into the action. He put the interests of the team above his own, and in that way helped them secure massive victories. His greatest performances often came in the playoffs. In Game Five of the 1968 Eastern Division Finals, he saved the Celtics from elimination by scoring 29 points, taking 9 rebounds, and making 10 assists. His performance in Game Seven was nearly as spectacular, and the Celtics became the first NBA team to win a playoff series after losing three of the first four games.

POSITIONS: SMALL FORWARD/SHOOTING GUARD
BORN: APRIL 8, 1940
DIED: APRIL 25, 2019
HEIGHT: 6 FT 5 IN
TEAM: BOSTON CELTICS (1962–78)

Allen Iverson was one of the bravest players in NBA history. He stood just six feet tall and weighed only 165 pounds, but he attacked the biggest and best defenders in the NBA without blinking an eye.

Iverson was born in Hampton, Virginia, in 1975. His mother, Ann Iverson, was only 15 years old when she had Allen, and she gave him her own last name after his father left her.

Iverson was known in his neighborhood for looking after the younger kids. His athletic abilities also became apparent early on, and he was a dual-sport athlete at Bethel High School. In football he played mainly as a quarterback, but he also took the field as a running back, kick returner, and defensive back. In basketball he played as a point guard. He led his football and basketball teams to the Virginia state championships and was named Associated Press High School Player of the Year in both sports. He also joined the Boo Williams AAU basketball team and won the 17-and-under AAU national championship.

His next stop was Georgetown University, which has always been known for developing great centers, like Patrick Ewing, Alonzo Mourning, and Dikembe Mutombo. But now it was time for a short point guard to lead the Hoyas. In his second year, Iverson took the team to the Big East Conference title and was named a First-Team All-American. He was Big East Defender of the Year in both his college seasons, and claims the Hoyas' highest career scoring average, at 22.9 points per game.

He was probably the best-known player to enter the 1996 NBA draft, and was chosen first, by the Philadelphia 76ers, making him the shortest player ever to be the first overall pick. Iverson immediately carved out his place in the NBA, averaging 23.5 points per game in his rookie year along with 7.5 assists. He only continued to improve from there, and his fifth NBA season was one of the best any guard ever had. He was named league MVP and All-Star Game MVP, and led the NBA in both scoring and steals. He took the Sixers all the way to the NBA finals, where they lost to the Los Angeles Lakers, led by the incredible duo of Shaquille O'Neal and Kobe Bryant.

Iverson is one of the league's greatest scorers in recent decades, averaging more than 30 points in four seasons. His achievement is all the more impressive given the style of play that was typical during his career: defenses were tighter, and the score was usually lower than it is now. Iverson set records as a defender, too, topping the league's stealing charts three times.

POSITIONS: POINT GUARD/SHOOTING GUARD/COMBO GUARD
BORN: JUNE 7, 1975
HEIGHT: 6 FT
TEAMS: PHILADELPHIA 76ERS (1996–2006), DENVER NUGGETS (2006–8), DETROIT PISTONS (2008–9), MEMPHIS GRIZZLIES (2009), PHILADELPHIA 76ERS (2009–10)

IVERSON

Earvin "Magic" Johnson changed the role of the point guard when he entered the NBA. He was intelligent on the court and quick to read situations, and he had exceptional ball-handling technique and passing ability for a man of his size. At 6'9" with a strong physique, he was unstoppable on fast breaks.

When Magic entered the NBA in 1979, many sportswriters thought he should play as a forward, but Lakers coach Jack McKinney decided to make him a point guard instead. For four seasons, Magic shared this position with Norm Nixon, a star in his own right, until the Lakers traded Nixon away so Magic could have it to himself.

Magic made a huge contribution to the team in his rookie season, averaging 18 points per game, with 7.7 rebounds and 7.3 assists. He was chosen for the Western Conference's starting lineup in the annual All-Star Game.

Magic was particularly excited to play alongside the Lakers' star, Kareem Abdul-Jabbar, the highest-scoring player in NBA history. The rookie point guard seemed to have a good influence on Abdul-Jabbar, who averaged a point more per game after Magic joined the team, despite playing fewer minutes.

However, in the sixth game of the 1980 finals against the Philadelphia 76ers, Abdul-Jabbar was out with a sprained ankle, and Magic was moved to the center position in his place. The talented rookie was unfazed by the challenge of playing a new position in the most important game of the season. He scored 42 points, took 15 rebounds, gave 7 assists, and made 3 steals, clinching the victory for the Lakers. Magic's performance in this deciding game is considered one of the best in NBA history, and he is still the only rookie to have been named Finals MVP.

Magic's career was eventually cut short by a startling diagnosis: in 1991, he announced that he had tested positive for HIV and would be retiring from basketball. In those days, HIV was considered almost a death sentence, and fans around the world were shocked to learn that one of the NBA's brightest stars had contracted the virus.

Although Magic had retired before the 1991–92 season began, fans voted him into the Western Conference's starting lineup for the 1992 All-Star Game. The NBA board decided to allow Magic to compete, but some players, like Karl Malone of the Utah Jazz, were concerned about the risk of HIV transmission. Shortly before All-Star Weekend, Magic's good friend, Isiah Thomas of the Detroit Pistons, called a player meeting and got his fellow All Stars to agree to let Magic play.

At the All-Star Game in Orlando, fans were exhilarated when Magic's name was announced before the game. As the crowd stood and applauded, Magic's opponents hugged him, with Isiah Thomas leading the way.

It was clear that Magic did not show up just to score himself. By the end of the third quarter, the West had a lead of 32 points, thanks to the magnificent passes that Magic had focused on feeding to his teammates. In the fourth quarter, he started to move outside the three-point line and scored two beautiful shots from there. On the other end, in defense, he guarded Isiah Thomas and Michael Jordan one after the other. The fans applauded Magic's dedication to defense, which is rare in All-Star Games.

The final offensive play was highly memorable. Magic was guarded by his good friend Isiah Thomas and decided to make a rainbow shot over him at the final whistle. The ball went straight in; it was Magic's third basket in as many shots. The fans were overjoyed and everyone celebrated—Magic's teammates and opponents alike.

POSITION: POINT GUARD
BORN: AUGUST 14, 1959
HEIGHT: 6 FT 9 IN
TEAM: LOS ANGELES LAKERS
(1979–91, 1996)

JOHNSON

JORDAN

Michael Jordan is widely considered to be the best basketball player of all time. Even his fellow superstars put him in a league of his own: "There's Michael Jordan and then there is the rest of us," Magic Johnson once said.

After three years of college ball with the North Carolina Tar Heels, Jordan entered the 1984 NBA draft and went to the Chicago Bulls as the third overall pick. The first overall pick was Hakeem Olajuwon, a legend in his own right, but the second was Sam Bowie, who went on to a disappointing and injury-plagued NBA career. Bowie being chosen over Jordan is considered one of the worst draft decisions in NBA history.

With the Bulls, Jordan instantly became a star and took a previously mediocre team to new heights. As a top scorer, he would make impressive leaps up to the basket and slam dunk like no one else, earning him the nickname "Air Jordan" (a name that Nike would borrow for the extremely popular line of sneakers it produced in collaboration with the superstar). In one exhibition game in Italy, Jordan even shattered the backboard glass with his impressive dunk. Soon everyone knew his name, and he became not just a basketball star but a global celebrity.

One of Jordan's most defining moments came in the 1989 playoffs. The Chicago Bulls were up against the Cleveland Cavaliers in Game Five of the Eastern Conference First Round series, and the Cavs were winning by one point with just three seconds left. But Jordan was quick on his feet. He received an inbound pass and then made a buzzer-beater shot, giving the Bulls a 101−100 victory. The Bulls won the series, and "the Shot" went down in NBA history.

Jordan eventually led the Bulls to three consecutive championship wins, in 1991, 1992, and 1993. Even though his career was at its height, Jordan decided he wanted a break from the game, and left the NBA in order to play a season of Minor League Baseball. It was a short retirement, though, and Jordan announced his return to professional basketball in 1995 with a famous two-word press release: "I'm back."

With Jordan on their team again, the Bulls made it to the 1995 playoffs. They lost in the Eastern Conference Semifinals that year, but they went on to win three more championships, in 1996, 1997, and 1998, giving Jordan a career total of six. His other honors include being named the NBA MVP five times, the NBA Finals MVP six times, and the All-Star Game MVP three times—not to mention being picked for the All-Star Team 14 times, the All-NBA First Team 10 times, and the NBA All-Defensive First Team nine times. To this day, he holds the NBA records for career regular scoring average (30.12 points per game) and career playoff scoring average (33.45 points per game). He was inducted into Basketball Hall of Fame not once, but twice—the first time for his individual career, and the second as part of the famous Dream Team that went to the 1992 Olympics.

Jordan's statistics and accolades are matched only by the popular acclaim he enjoyed throughout his career. More than anyone else, he is responsible for making basketball a worldwide sport. Today's stars may have followers on social media, but Michael Jordan had followers in real life: thousands of fans would wait outside the hotels where the Bulls stayed, hoping to see their basketball idol.

POSITIONS: SHOOTING GUARD/SMALL FORWARD
BORN: FEBRUARY 17, 1963
HEIGHT: 6 FT 6 IN
TEAMS: CHICAGO BULLS (1984–93, 1995–98),
WASHINGTON WIZARDS (2001–3)

MALONE

Of all the NBA players in history, the one his opponents probably *least* wanted to get in a rebounding battle with was Moses Malone. He led the league in rebounding in six seasons, five of them in a row (1981–85), an achievement that earned him the nickname "Chairman of the Boards."

Malone was born in Petersburg, Virginia. His father was 5'6" and his mother 5'2", but Malone was much taller and became a standout on the Petersburg High School basketball team. In his junior and senior years, the team went undefeated and won back-to-back state championships. Malone was highly sought after by college coaches, and some 300 coaches and scouts came out to watch him play in his senior year.

He signed a letter of intent to play for the University of Maryland but also entered the 1974 ABA draft. When he was picked by Utah Stars of the ABA, Malone—who had grown up in poverty—seized the opportunity to turn pro right out of high school. He was the first basketball player of the modern era to do so.

When Malone joined the ABA, talks were already underway to merge it with the NBA, as some ABA teams were struggling financially. In fact, after Malone's rookie year, in which he scored 22.7 points per game and took 17.5 rebounds, the Utah Stars folded and he was traded to the Spirits of St. Louis.

Finally, in 1976, the leagues merged. St. Louis was one of the teams that was not absorbed into the NBA, so Malone went into the ABA Dispersal Draft. He was first selected by the Portland Trail Blazers, who traded him to the Buffalo Braves. There he appeared in two games, but with the prospect of only limited playing time, he managed to get transferred to the Houston Rockets.

Malone's career took off with the Rockets. In Houston, he was reunited with his old coach from the Utah Stars, Tom Nissalke, who helped him make the transition from power forward to center. Malone had been quite slim when he first went pro, but now he was more muscular and could make himself felt. He took his offensive rebounding to a new level and was twice named league MVP. Presumably the Blazers and the Braves (who became the Clippers in 1978) had many occasions to regret giving him up.

Then, in 1982, the Rockets franchise was sold, and the new owners agreed to trade Malone to the Philadelphia 76ers for a first round draft pick. This was an advantageous deal for the Sixers, who had lost to the Lakers 4–2 in the finals and needed Malone's help around the basket.

Malone joined an outstanding core at the Sixers, including Julius Erving, Maurice Cheeks, Andrew Toney, and Bobby Jones, among others. The team was unstoppable in the regular season and arrived at the finals full of confidence. Malone famously predicted in his Southern accent that Philadelphia would go "fo, fo, fo"—that is, sweep all three rounds of the finals. They ending up going four, *five*, four (losing one game to the Bucks), but it was still a spectacular performance. Malone was named league MVP for the second year in a row and the third time in his career. He led the league in rebounds, with 15.3 per game, and scored 24.5 points per game. There was no denying that he was one of the best inside players the NBA had ever seen.

POSITIONS: CENTER/POWER FORWARD
BORN: MARCH 23, 1955
DIED: SEPTEMBER 13, 2015
HEIGHT: 6 FT 10 IN
TEAMS: UTAH STARS (1974–75), SPIRITS OF ST. LOUIS (1975–76), BUFFALO
BRAVES (1976), HOUSTON ROCKETS (1976–82), PHILADELPHIA 76ERS
(1982–86), WASHINGTON BULLETS (1986–88), ATLANTA HAWKS (1988–91),
MILWAUKEE BUCKS (1991–93), PHILADELPHIA 76ERS (1993–94),
SAN ANTONIO SPURS (1994–95)

NASH

Steve Nash has an unusual background for an NBA legend: He was born in South Africa to a Welsh mother and an English father and was raised in Victoria, British Columbia. He grew up playing soccer and ice hockey, and did not give basketball a try until he was 12 or 13 years old.

But the game hooked him immediately, and he soon vowed to his mother that he would be a star in the NBA. In high school, he played soccer and rugby but excelled most of all at basketball. In his senior year at St. Michaels University School in Victoria, he led the school to a provincial championship and was named player of the year in British Columbia.

Nash's high school coach tried his best to interest American colleges in his star point guard. At this point, in the early 1990s, not many Canadian players had made it to the United States, and Nash received many rejection letters. But one coach, Dick Davey of Santa Clara University, was intrigued by Nash's audition videotapes, and after he saw him play in person, he immediately offered him a scholarship.

Nash led the Santa Clara Broncos for four years. In his first season, the team reached the NCAA tournament for the first time in five years and beat the University of Arizona in the first round, a notable upset. But in the second round the team lost to Temple. The Broncos went to the NCAA tournament twice more during Nash's college career, and he was named West Coast Conference Men's Player of the Year two seasons in a row.

After graduating from Santa Clara University, Nash fulfilled his promise to his mother and entered the NBA in the 1996 draft. The Phoenix Suns selected him as the 15th pick in the first round. Suns fans booed their team for picking a comparatively unknown player from a smaller college conference. Eventually they would have cause to change their minds, but not right away—Nash got off to a slow start and only scored 3.3 points per game in his rookie year. After his second season, he was traded to the Dallas Mavericks.

In his six years with the Mavericks, Nash developed into one of the league's most formidable point guards. Then, in 2004, he returned to the Suns as a free agent. Once again some fans questioned the acquisition, because Nash was now on a big contract and would have to play very well to justify it.

But Nash proved all his doubters wrong. Under coach Mike D'Antoni, he helped changed the offensive game in the NBA. The team's strategy was called Seven Seconds or Less, referring to the time in which they tried to complete their attacks. Although Nash never managed to win an NBA title with the Suns, he was named league MVP two years in a row, in 2005 and 2006. He is one of only 12 players in NBA history to earn this distinction.

POSITION: POINT GUARD
BORN: FEBRUARY 7, 1974
HEIGHT: 6 FT 3 IN
TEAMS: PHOENIX SUNS (1996–98), DALLAS MAVERICKS (1998–2004),
PHOENIX SUNS (2004–12), LOS ANGELES LAKERS (2012–15)

"You must now decide whether you want to play against the best in the world or just stay a local hero in Germany. If you choose the latter, we will stop training immediately, because nobody can prevent that anymore. But if you want to play against the best, we have to train on a daily basis." That is what coach Holger Geschwindner said to a 16-year-old Dirk Nowitzki. At that point Geschwindner had coached Nowitzki for a year with amazing results, and it was already clear that the promising young player could make it to the NBA.

Nowitzki came from a family of athletes. His mother, Helga, had played basketball for the West German national team, and his father, Jörg-Werner, had played professional handball. Dirk and his older sister Silke played multiple sports growing up. Silke was a strong track and field competitor who later played professional basketball in Germany. Dirk was a nationally ranked junior tennis player and also played team handball like his father. But because he was a foot taller than most of his peers, he eventually followed his mother and his sister onto the basketball court.

Nowitzki had been playing for about two years when he attracted the attention of Geschwindner, who had captained the West German basketball team in the 1972 Olympics. Geschwindner initially offered to coach Nowitzki two to three times per week and focused on technical drills to improve his shooting and ball handling. He avoided all tactical coaching and also discouraged Nowitzki from lifting weights. Off the court, Geschwindner encouraged Nowitzki to play a musical instrument and read books, in order to become a more well-rounded person.

Nowitzki certainly had an interesting mentor—in fact, Geschwindner has attracted worldwide attention for the unconventional basketball camp he runs for young players. After skeptical observers derided his techniques as nonsense, he proudly dubbed the camp the Institute of Applied Nonsense. Among other things, he has had young players row a boat together, play soccer with members of the German national team, dance, and dribble the ball to the rhythm of jazz music. Geschwindner has also calculated the optimal angle of a jump shot, which he says is 60 degrees.

When training young athletes, the most important thing is to think long-term, to see what kind of players they can become in the future and aim for that. Geschwindner could have cut corners in Nowitzki's training by having him lift weights and sacrifice some of his agility and technique in exchange for strength. Instead, he stuck to his plan and gave Nowitzki a unique technical foundation.

No doubt Nowitzki sometimes questioned his mentor's methods when he first entered the NBA at age 20, because physically he was not quite ready for the fight. He was overwhelmed by other, stronger power forwards, his defensive play was criticized, and he seemed generally ill at ease on the court.

But, slowly, Nowitzki's technique, agility, and resilience began to pay off. He went from scoring 8.2 points per game in his rookie year to 17.5 points in his second year. He averaged over 20 points per game for 12 consecutive seasons. He was named league MVP in 2007 and Finals MVP in 2011, the year he led the Dallas Mavericks to the championship.

Dirk Nowitzki was the fourth German to play in the NBA and by far the best. In fact, he is probably the best European player in NBA history, and one of the greatest power forwards of all time.

POSITIONS: POWER FORWARD/CENTER
BORN: JUNE 19, 1978
HEIGHT: 7 FT
TEAM: DALLAS MAVERICKS (1998–2019)

NOWITZKI

OLAJUWON

Hakeem Olajuwon was born in Lagos, Nigeria, where his parents owned a cement business. He grew up playing soccer and handball, and didn't touch a basketball until he was 15, when he was asked to play for his high school in a local tournament. The tall, athletic youth came to the attention of coach Rich Mills, who recruited him to Nigeria's junior national basketball team.

Olajuwon's skills quickly advanced to the point where playing college ball in the US became a possibility, and in 1980 he flew to Texas to attend the University of Houston. After a slow start, his college career took off in a big way: he and his teammates, including Clyde Drexler, made it to the NCAA championship game two years in a row with an energetic, freewheeling style of play that led a local sportswriter to dub them "Phi Slama Jama," the "slam-dunk fraternity."

The Rockets chose Olajuwon as the first overall pick in the 1984 NBA draft, allowing him to stay in his adopted city of Houston. (This was same draft in which Michael Jordan went to the Chicago Bulls as the third overall pick.)

Olajuwon's long career with the Rockets peaked in the mid-nineties. He led them to back-to-back championships in 1994 and 1995, and in 1994, he was named regular season MVP, Finals MVP, and Defensive Player of the Year.

Over his 18-year NBA career, Olajuwon averaged 21.8 points per game, 11.1 rebounds, and 3.1 shots blocked. He led the league for two seasons in rebounds and three seasons in blocked shots. In fact, no player in NBA history has blocked more shots.

Olajuwon was nicknamed "the Dream" because one of his college coaches said he dunked the ball so effortlessly that it seemed as if he were in a dream. He had unique footwork around the basket, and his favorite move was the "Dream Shake," an agile, dance-like series of steps that left defenders bewildered.

Olajuwon is a devout Muslim, and in 1995 he began observing Ramadan fasts even on game days. When he had an afternoon game, this meant he had to play without taking a single sip of water. But Olajuwon did not view this as a hardship: rather, he has said that his faith made him a stronger player, particularly during Ramadan.

POSITION: CENTER
BORN: JANUARY 21, 1963
HEIGHT: 7 FT
TEAMS: HOUSTON ROCKETS (1984–2001), TORONTO RAPTORS (2001–2)

O'NEAL

Shaquille O'Neal—known around the world as "Shaq"—stands 7'1", and at his best, he was unstoppable on the court. Defenders bounced off of him, and he dunked whenever he felt like it—occasionally breaking the backboard.

After three standout seasons at Louisiana State University, Shaq was chosen by the Orlando Magic as the first overall pick in the 1992 NBA draft. He was the young expansion franchise's first superstar, and—with the help of guard Penny Hardaway, whom the team picked up in the 1993 draft—he brought the Magic to the NBA finals in 1995.

Orlando fans were dealt a harsh blow in 1996, however, when Shaq moved to the Lakers. Shaq had his best seasons in Los Angeles, propelling the Lakers to three titles in a row, in 2000, 2001, and 2002, alongside a young Kobe Bryant. Shaq and Kobe's relationship was often strained, but as Shaq himself put it, they were like brothers.

In the finals series of 2000–2002, Shaq averaged 35.9 points, 15.2 rebounds, 2.9 blocks, and 3.5 assists. It is worth repeating that these were his statistics in the NBA finals, the highest level of basketball in the world. No one could stop him, although many tried. It was common for teams to have a few big and heavy centers on the bench who would take turns fouling O'Neal in order to send him to the free-throw line, where he often had a difficult time making shots. This strategy was called "Hack-a-Shaq."

After Shaq left the Lakers, he went from team to team. His longest stay was with the Miami Heat. He won the NBA finals with them in 2006—his fourth title, and the Heat's first. Short stints in Phoenix, Cleveland, and Boston followed, but Shaq was increasingly plagued by injuries and retired in 2011, after 19 years in the league.

Shaq was a four-time NBA champion, three-time Finals MVP, and one-time league MVP. He averaged almost 24 points and 11 rebounds per game over his career, and was the league's top scorer in two seasons. He is the only player in NBA history to have averaged more than 20 points and 10 rebounds per game in 13 different seasons. In 10 seasons he had the best shot percentage in the league, because he dunked so often. But among NBA players who have taken at least 2,000 free throws in their careers, he has the third-worst free throw percentage. Shaq himself attributes this to a mental block, because his free-throw accuracy was much better in practice.

POSITION: CENTER
BORN: MARCH 6, 1972
HEIGHT: 7 FT 1 IN
TEAMS: ORLANDO MAGIC (1992–96), LOS ANGELES LAKERS (1996–2004),
MIAMI HEAT (2004–8), PHOENIX SUNS (2008–9), CLEVELAND CAVALIERS
(2009–10), BOSTON CELTICS (2010–11)

PIPPEN

Scottie Pippen's versatility always made him a fan favorite. As Michael Jordan's best teammate, he was a key part of one of the greatest superpowers in NBA history and played a role in bringing basketball to a world stage.

Pippen was born in Hamburg, Arkansas, and had 11 older siblings. The entire family was tall—his father was 6'1", and his mother 6'0"—but Scottie was the tallest. He played point guard on his high school basketball team and was considered a clever player in that position. However, he did not receive any scholarship offers, so he began his college career as a walk-on at the University of Central Arkansas. There he grew as a player, including in a literal sense: he was 6'1" when he left high school, and 6'8" when he left college. Since he had played as a point guard all his life, he had great ball handling and vision, skills that would help him later on.

The University of Central Arkansas played not in the NCAA but in the NAIA, an athletic association for smaller colleges, and they usually did not receive much media attention. But word of Pippen's talent got out, and he was the fifth pick in the first round of the 1987 NBA draft. He was chosen initially by the Seattle SuperSonics, who traded him to the Chicago Bulls in a draft-night deal.

With the Bulls, Pippen built a reputation as an amazingly athletic and team-focused small forward. He was selected for the NBA All-Defensive First Team eight times in a row and was in the NBA All-Star Game seven times, winning the All-Star MVP trophy in 1994. Pippen played close to Jordan, and they were considered the best one-two punch in the league; together they were instrumental to the Bulls' two championship three-peats, in 1991–93 and 1996–98.

Pippen's triumphs extended to the international stage as well. He was the first player in history to twice win an NBA championship ring and an Olympic gold medal in the same year, in 1992 and 1996. After his second Olympic outing, he was named USA Basketball Male Athlete of the Year.

Looking back, Pippen is sometimes underrated because he played alongside Michael Jordan. But Pippen's own accomplishments easily qualify him as one of the best small forwards in the history of the league.

POSITION: SMALL FORWARD
BORN: SEPTEMBER 25, 1965
HEIGHT: 6 FT 8 IN
TEAMS: CHICAGO BULLS (1987–98), HOUSTON ROCKETS (1999), PORTLAND TRAIL BLAZERS (1999–2003), CHICAGO BULLS (2003–4)

ROBERTSON

To get a triple-double—a double-digit number of points, rebounds, and assists—in one game is an achievement for most players. Oscar Robertson took it to another level when he averaged a triple-double for a whole season. As a player, he was ahead of his time: he had everything that today's NBA coaches would want in a point guard. He was tall for his position, had a great eye for creative play, and took a lot of rebounds. A point guard who can rebound well is a real asset, because then the team can immediately transition to a fast break.

Robertson grew up in a segregated housing project in Indianapolis, Indiana, and his childhood was marked by poverty and racism. Still, he showed great promise on the basketball court from an early age. At the all-Black Crispus Attucks High School in Indianapolis, he led the basketball team to two state championships in a row. In his senior year, the Crispus Attucks team not only won the championship but compiled a perfect record, and Robertson was named Indiana Mr. Basketball.

He was sought after by college coaches and chose to play for the University of Cincinnati. In his three seasons with the Cincinnati Bearcats, he averaged 33.8 points per game, which is the third-highest average in college basketball history. Robertson set numerous NCAA and school records and led the Bearcats to two Final Four appearances, but failed to win a championship.

After leaving college, Robertson was selected for the US national team that went to the 1960 Olympics. This team is remembered as perhaps the best amateur lineup in basketball history: Robertson co-captained the team with Jerry West, and nine of their ten teammates went on to careers in the NBA. Robertson returned home with a gold medal and entered the 1960 NBA draft, in which he was chosen by the Cincinnati Royals as a territorial pick.

As a professional, Robertson continued to dominate his opponents. He made a habit of reaching triple-doubles: in fact, his statistics from his first five NBA seasons taken together average out to a triple-double. Robertson played with the Royals for 10 years, but they never managed to win the championship, despite his own outstanding performance.

Then, in 1970, Robertson was traded to the Milwaukee Bucks for two players of a decidedly lesser caliber, in what is regarded as one of the worst player exchanges of all times. It has been said that Royals coach Bob Cousy made the trade because he was jealous that Robertson had broken many of the records Cousy had previously set as a player.

But it was with the Bucks that Robertson managed to finally win an NBA championship, in 1971. In Milwaukee, he played alongside a young Kareem Abdul-Jabbar; they formed one of the best double acts in NBA history.

Oscar Robertson, nicknamed "the Big O," influenced the game in many ways. He was an innovator who is remembered as the first "big guard" and is credited with inventing the head fake and the fadeaway jump shot. Robertson also set the benchmark for versatility: He was one of the best scorers the league has ever seen, but he was also great at finding his teammates with passes. He was a fantastic free-throw shooter and twice led the league in free-throw percentages. In other words, he was an all-around great.

POSITION: POINT GUARD
BORN: NOVEMBER 24, 1938
HEIGHT: 6 FT 5 IN
TEAMS: CINCINNATI ROYALS (1960–69),
MILWAUKEE BUCKS (1970–74)

ROBINSON

In high school, David Robinson was a star student before he was a star athlete. He only joined the basketball team in his senior year, after he experienced a growth spurt that took him from 5'9" to 6'6".

The son of a Navy veteran, Robinson decided to attend the United States Naval Academy. When he was admitted to the academy, he was exactly at the maximum height allowed by the Navy. But then he kept growing, all the way to 7'1", and the Navy basketball team found themselves with a tall center.

The Midshipmen did extremely well with Robinson on board. His junior year happened to be the first season in which the NCAA recorded statistics for blocked shots. In that season, 1985–86, Robinson racked up 207 blocks, which is still the all-time record in the NCAA.

After Robinson graduated from the Naval Academy, he was picked first in the 1987 NBA draft, by the San Antonio Spurs—but before he could play for the NBA, he had to complete the military service required of all service academy graduates. Here Robinson's towering stature presented a problem: he was too tall to serve safely in the confined spaces of Navy ships and submarines. As a compromise, the Secretary of the Navy gave him special permission to serve his active duty on land, in the Navy's Civil Engineer Corps, and for a period of two years rather than the usual five.

Robinson joined the Spurs after this two-year hiatus, and he did not miss a beat. He averaged 24.3 points and 12 rebounds per game in his first season. He was named Rookie of the Year, and not only because of his statistics: the Spurs won 35 more games than in their previous season, a record improvement in the history of the game.

Robinson—or "the Admiral," as he was called due to his Navy service—was the NBA's top rebounder in 1991, top shot-blocker in 1992, Defender of the Year in 1992, top scorer in 1994, and MVP in 1995. He went to 10 All-Star Games, and he was named to the All-NBA First Team four times. To top off a great career, he won two NBA championships, in 1999 and 2003.

POSITION: CENTER
BORN: AUGUST 6, 1965
HEIGHT: 7 FT 1 IN
TEAM: SAN ANTONIO SPURS (1989–2003)

Bill Russell won a record 11 titles in 13 years in the NBA, and he is considered one of the best defenders in the history of the game. In his honor, the NBA Finals MVP trophy was renamed the Bill Russell NBA Finals Most Valuable Player Award. But, surprisingly, this all-time legend had a rocky start in basketball.

Russell was born in West Monroe, Louisiana, and moved with his family to Oakland, California, when he was eight years old. He was considered a promising athlete, a fast runner with an impressive jump and big hands, but he was slow to master the fundamentals of basketball and was cut from the team at Herbert Hoover Junior High School. At McClymonds High School he was almost cut again, but coach George Powles saw his potential and helped him work on his skills.

Russell soon developed innovative defensive techniques. At that time, players were told to stay flat-footed when they were on the defense, to help their reaction times. But Russell pioneered an aerial defense, jumping up to block shots. He also began to memorize the movements of his opponents when he saw them play, so he would know how to counter them on the court.

This level of basketball intelligence and intuition was rarely seen in such a young player—so, despite his relative weakness on the offense, Russell earned a scholarship to the University of San Francisco. The USF coach, Phil Woolpert, believed that skin color should play no role in picking the team, and the USF Dons were the first NCAA squad to have three Black players in their starting lineup: Russell, Hal Perry, and K. C. Jones. However, the team had to endure much racial abuse. At a college tournament in Oklahoma City, USF's Black players were barred from the city's hotels. The entire team decided to stay in a college dorm instead, an experience that Russell recalled as bringing them closer together.

At USF, Russell continued to improve his defensive game. Instead of guarding the opposing center closely, as was then the custom, he kept a certain distance. This allowed him to intervene and block shots from other offensive players, but he also had the speed to find the opposing center again if the offense continued.

Russell was the second pick in the 1956 NBA draft and went to the Boston Celtics in a draft-day trade. (The Celtics also drafted his USF teammate K. C. Jones.) Russell was joining an amazing attacking team that had not been as successful in defense. But, as the Celtics' coach, the legendary Red Auerbach, had hoped, Russell completely eliminated this weakness. Even as a rookie, he played an integral part of the team that led the Celtics to their first championship in 1957.

In Russell's second season with the Celtics, he was named league MVP, but the team fell short of another championship. In the years from 1959 to 1966, however, the Celtics won a record eight championships in a row. When Red Auerbach decided to retire from coaching in 1966, Russell was appointed player-coach. This made him the first Black coach in the history of the NBA. With Russell at the helm, the Celtics won titles in 1968 and 1969.

Russell is one of only two NBA player-coaches to have won a championship, and the only one to have won multiple titles. He was also league MVP five times, rebound leader four times, and an NBA All-Star 12 times.

RUSSELL

POSITION: CENTER
BORN: FEBRUARY 12, 1934
HEIGHT: 6 FT 10 IN
TEAM: BOSTON CELTICS (1956–69)

THOMAS

In the era of physical basketball, a small but fierce point guard stood his ground and led one of the toughest teams in NBA history to two titles. This 6'1" powerhouse, Isiah Thomas, was born and raised in Chicago and started playing basketball when he was only three years old. He immediately attracted attention for his ball-handling skills, which he would show off at halftime at Catholic Youth Organization games.

Thomas played for St. Joseph's High School in Westchester, Illinois, and led the team to the state finals in his junior year. He was considered one of the top college prospects in the country and had many schools to choose from. Finally, in consultation with his mother, he decided to play for the tough but respected Bobby Knight, who coached the Indiana Hoosiers. Thomas had been warned that Knight was a strict disciplinarian with a quick temper, but his mother thought Thomas would benefit from Knight's discipline. In the end, it turned out to be a good choice.

Thomas played two seasons for Indiana and established himself as the leader of the team even in his first year. In fact, Knight adapted his style of play to Thomas: he was just such a dominant factor on the squad that Knight had to get everything he could out of him.

In his first year with Indiana, Thomas led the Hoosiers to the Big Ten Championship and to the Sweet Sixteen of the NCAA tournament. Then, in his second year, Thomas and Indiana went all the way and won the NCAA title. Thomas was named NCAA Final Four Most Outstanding Player and a Consensus First Team All-American.

These accolades gave Thomas a high profile coming into the 1981 NBA draft. He was the second pick overall, after his future teammate Mark Aquirre, and went to the Detroit Pistons.

At that time, the Pistons were struggling. The prior season, they had won only 21 games and lost 61. In Thomas's first season, that record improved by 18 wins, and the talented rookie averaged 17.1 points per game. The Pistons continued to improve in the following seasons, with Thomas serving as team leader and Joe Dumars, Bill Laimbeer, and Rick Mahorn filling out the core. In 1986, the Pistons also brought Dennis Rodman and Adrian Dantley on board.

Dantley, who had averaged more than 30 points per game in four of his seven seasons with the Utah Jazz, was supposed to give the Pistons the extra edge they needed to make it to the top. But Dantley clashed with Thomas and other Pistons players and coaches, and he was traded to the Mavericks in February 1989 for Mark Aguirre.

With the addition of Aguirre, the Pistons finally had all ingredients in place, and they took the NBA championship in 1989 and 1990. Thomas remained the star of the team, who became known as the "Bad Boys" for their aggressive style of play. When Thomas retired, he held the Pistons' record for career points and assists. He also held the scoring record for a single quarter in the NBA finals, having scored 25 points against the Lakers in one quarter in 1988.

POSITION: POINT GUARD
BORN: APRIL 30, 1961
HEIGHT: 6 FT 1 IN
TEAM: DETROIT PISTONS (1981–94)

Dwyane Wade is a good example of a late bloomer. This amazing shooting guard continued to develop his game after entering the league and then peaked on the biggest stage of them all, the NBA finals. But his journey had a very rocky beginning.

Wade was born in Chicago. His parents divorced when he was young, and at first he and his older sister, Tragil, lived with their mother. The siblings were forced to rely on each other while their mother struggled with drug addiction. When Wade was eight, he and Tragil went to live with his father and stepmother.

Wade played both football and basketball at Harold L. Richards High School in Oak Lawn, a suburb of Chicago. At first he was more promising in football, as a wide receiver. But then he had a growth spurt before his junior year, and it became clear which sport he should focus on. He was already a technically proficient basketball player, and when height and strength were added to the mix, he became unstoppable. He set school records in points and steals, and attracted the attention of college scouts.

Because of his poor academic record, though, Wade received only three scholarship offers, from Illinois State, DePaul, and Marquette. He chose Marquette but had to sit out his freshman year because he was academically ineligible to play under NCAA rules. However, with intensive studying and tutoring, he became eligible to play in his sophomore year, and he never looked back from there.

In his junior year, 2002–3, Wade brought Marquette to the Final Four for the first time since 1977. He did so in memorable fashion, with a victory against the top-seeded Kentucky Wildcats in which he totaled 29 points, 11 rebounds, and 11 assists. This was only the fourth triple-double in NCAA tournament history. It was a performance that skyrocketed Wade to stardom,

and he became the fifth pick in the 2003 NBA draft, which is considered one of the strongest draft classes of all time. (Also in the top five picks that year were LeBron James, Carmelo Anthony, and Chris Bosh.)

Wade was selected by the Miami Heat, and this turned out to be one of the best decisions in the history of the franchise. He scored 16.2 points per game in his rookie year but really became a dominant force in his second year, when he scored 24.1 points and gave 6.8 assists.

In his third year, Wade led the Heat all the way to the 2006 NBA championship. His performance in the finals was spectacular. The Heat faced the Dallas Mavericks, who won the first two games in the series. But in games three, four, and five, Wade scored 42, 36, and 43 points. In the sixth game, he again scored 36 points and secured the title for the Heat. Overall he averaged 34.7 points per game in the series and became the fifth-youngest player in history to be named Finals MVP.

In 2010, LeBron James and Chris Bosh both joined the Heat. With James, Bosh, and Wade—aka "the Big Three"—in the starting lineup, the Heat became the top draw in the NBA. The Big Three won back-to-back titles for Miami in 2012 and 2013. Although Wade was sharing the spotlight now, he still played an important part. He scored 22.6 points per game in the 2012 finals against the Oklahoma City Thunder. And the next year he recovered from an injury-plagued season to score 19.6 points per game in the finals against the San Antonio Spurs.

In addition to his three NBA titles, Wade was the league's top scorer in 2009 and a 13-time NBA All-Star. He won the admiration of fans for the way he played the game with sophistication, daring, and respect.

WADE

POSITIONS: POINT GUARD/SHOOTING GUARD
BORN: JANUARY 17, 1982
HEIGHT: 6 FT 4 IN
TEAMS: MIAMI HEAT (2003–2016), CHICAGO
BULLS (2016–17), CLEVELAND CAVALIERS
(2017–18), MIAMI HEAT (2018–19)

WEST

If you've seen the NBA logo, you've seen a picture of Jerry West: the logo is based on a photo of him dribbling. However, the NBA board concealed this fact when the logo premiered in 1971, because they wanted to "institutionalize rather than individualize" the league.

Still, you must be quite the basketball player if your photo is turned into the logo of the top basketball league in the world. And West was indeed one of the all-time greats. He was an NBA champion and an Olympic gold medalist, and after his retirement he had a distinguished career as a coach and an executive.

West grew up in rural West Virginia, where he led East Bank High School to the state championship in his senior year, on March 24, 1956. In honor of this achievement, the school temporarily changed its name to "West Bank High School" on March 24 of every year. This tradition lasted until the school closed in 1999.

West was recruited by dozens of colleges, but he decided to stay close to home and play for West Virginia University. In his junior year, he led the team all the way to the NCAA finals. Although the West Virginia Mountaineers lost by one point to the California Golden Bears, West was named the Most Outstanding Player of the Final Four. When he graduated from WVU in 1960, he held almost every school record.

In the 1960 NBA draft, West was selected by the Minneapolis Lakers with the second pick. (The team would relocate to Los Angeles in 1961.) The only player picked ahead of him was Oscar Robertson, who also went on to become one of the best guards in history. Before they joined their respective NBA teams, West and Robertson co-captained the US national team that won the gold medal at the 1960 Olympics. That US team is remembered as one of the greatest amateur squads of all time—at the Olympics, their average winning margin was 42 points!

West stayed with the Lakers for his entire NBA career. He was one of the best shooters in the league for as long as he played, and in four seasons he averaged more than 30 points per game. In the 1969–70 season, he became the first player over the age of 30 to average more than 30 points per game. Even today, there are still only seven players who can claim this distinction.

West reached the NBA finals a total of nine times but had to endure eight losses at that stage of the competition—six of them to Bill Russell's Celtics. His sole NBA championship came in the Lakers' epic 1971–72 season, in which they achieved a 33-game winning streak—still the league record.

As a player, West had multiple strong points. He often scored from long shots and would have accumulated even more points if he had played after the three-point line was introduced. He was also an outstanding defender who excelled at stealing the ball. For most of his playing career, there were no statistics for steals, but Wilt Chamberlain has said West stole as many balls in a month as the players who came after him stole in a year.

POSITIONS: POINT GUARD/SHOOTING GUARD
BORN: MAY 28, 1938
HEIGHT: 6 FT 3 IN
TEAM: LOS ANGELES LAKERS (1960–74)

WILKINS

Dominique Wilkins was born in Paris while his father was stationed there with the US Air Force. This forward with a French first name would go on to be a nine-time NBA All-Star and one of the league's most acrobatic players—although he would have to go to another continent to win a championship.

Wilkins grew up in Washington, North Carolina, where he led his high school to back-to-back state championships. He was recruited to the University of Georgia, where he earned the nickname "the Human Highlight Film" for his amazing dunks.

Three great forwards entered the 1982 NBA draft. James Worthy was selected first, Terry Cummings second, and Dominique Wilkins third. Wilkins was drafted by the Utah Jazz, but the cash-strapped team traded him to the Atlanta Hawks for two players and $1 million, in what turned out to be one of the most lopsided deals ever.

In Atlanta, Wilkins was part of a strong team that generally did well in the regular season: in four consecutive years, they won more than 50 games per season. But they never managed to get far in the postseason. Their best year was 1988, when they made it to the Eastern Conference Semifinals against the Boston Celtics. The series went on for seven games, and the deciding match was historic: Wilkins had a 47-point game and went basket for basket with Larry Bird in the fourth quarter, until Bird finally got the last one in, giving the Celtics a 118–116 win.

Some people though Wilkins's career was over after he ruptured his Achilles tendon in the 1991–92 season, but he proved them wrong, coming back in the next season to score an average of 29.9 points per game for the Hawks. In all, Wilkins managed to average at least 25 points for 10 seasons in a row.

In the middle of the 1993–94 season, Wilkins was traded to the Los Angeles Clippers. The transfer attracted attention because the Hawks were at the top of their conference when it took place, and Wilkins was the team's highest scorer. In fact, this was the only time a conference-leading NBA team has ever traded its top scorer after the All-Star break.

After finishing the 1993–94 season with the Clippers, Wilkins went to the Celtics, who were in a rebuilding phase. He scored 19 points per game and helped take the Celtics to the playoffs, but the team lost to the Orlando Magic in the first round.

Wilkins then left the Celtics for another team on another continent, but he kept the color green. Panathinaikos, one of Europe's most famous basketball teams, lured Wilkins to Greece with a rich contract, a four-story marble villa, a maid, and two cars. They even paid Wilkins's Greek taxes for him. Initially it was a difficult adjustment, and Wilkins clashed with his coach. But he went on to excel with Panathinaikos, leading the team to the EuroLeague championship and the Greek Cup. He was named MVP of both the EuroLeague Final Four and the Greek Cup Final.

After his one season in Greece, Wilkins continued to travel, spending a season with the San Antonio Spurs and a season in Italy. He spent the final season of his career with the Orlando Magic, where he played alongside his brother Gerard, who himself had a 14-year career in the NBA.

POSITION: SMALL FORWARD

BORN: JANUARY 12, 1960

HEIGHT: 6 FT 8 IN

TEAMS: ATLANTA HAWKS (1982–94), LOS ANGELES CLIPPERS (1994), BOSTON CELTICS (1994–95), SAN ANTONIO SPURS (1996–97), ORLANDO MAGIC (1998–99)

YAO

Yao Ming might be one of the biggest what-ifs in the history of the NBA. Standing 7'6", he still played the game of basketball with incredible finesse. He had a beautiful jump shot and an array of moves around the basket. He was on track to become one of the best centers of his generation before injuries derailed his career.

Yao's parents were both professional basketball players. His father was 6'7" and his mother 6'3", so it was no surprise that Yao weighed 11 pounds at birth, more than twice as much as the average Chinese newborn.

Yao was simply made for basketball. And on top of his physical gifts, he had a relentless drive to improve his game. He tried out for the Shanghai Sharks of the Chinese Basketball Association when he was only 13. To make the cut, he practiced for 10 hours a day at the Sharks' training camp. Yao played for the Sharks' junior team for four seasons before being promoted to the senior team. In his second season with the senior team, he broke his foot, foreshadowing the many foot injuries he would suffer over the course of his career.

Yao recovered to lead the Sharks to the CBA finals in his third and fourth seasons. Both times they lost to the Bayi Rockets, then the dominant team in the league. But in his fifth season, the Sharks again faced off against the Rockets in the finals—and won. Yao was voted league MVP, and at age 21, he had reached the pinnacle of basketball in his home country.

He decided to enter the 2002 NBA draft, but this was not an easy process, since he had to follow strict rules set by the Chinese authorities. For instance, he had to agree to honor certain commitments to play for the Chinese national team, regardless of the NBA schedule. Then the Chinese Basketball Association ruled that Yao would not be allowed to enter the 2002 draft unless he was drafted by the Houston Rockets with the first overall pick.

Yao's representatives managed to convince the CBA that the Rockets would draft him, and Yao finally got permission to enter the draft on the day it took place. Yao became the first number one draft pick who had never played basketball in the United States.

Yao's NBA career was slow to take off. He didn't score in his first game, and it took time for him to get used to the physical style of play. However, he still managed to average 13.5 points and 8.2 rebounds in his rookie year, and his numbers only improved from there. Even as he ascended to true NBA stardom, though, he began to accumulate foot injuries and miss games.

His injuries finally forced him to retire at age 31, after eight seasons in the NBA. He finished with career statistics of 19 points, 9.2 rebounds, and 1.9 blocks per game. Yao was not only a great basketball player whose career was cut short by injuries; he was also an ambassador for the game. His stature, both literally and figuratively, has helped basketball achieve its present status as the most popular sport in China.

POSITION: CENTER
BORN: SEPTEMBER 12, 1980
HEIGHT: 7 FT 6 IN
TEAM: HOUSTON ROCKETS (2002–11)

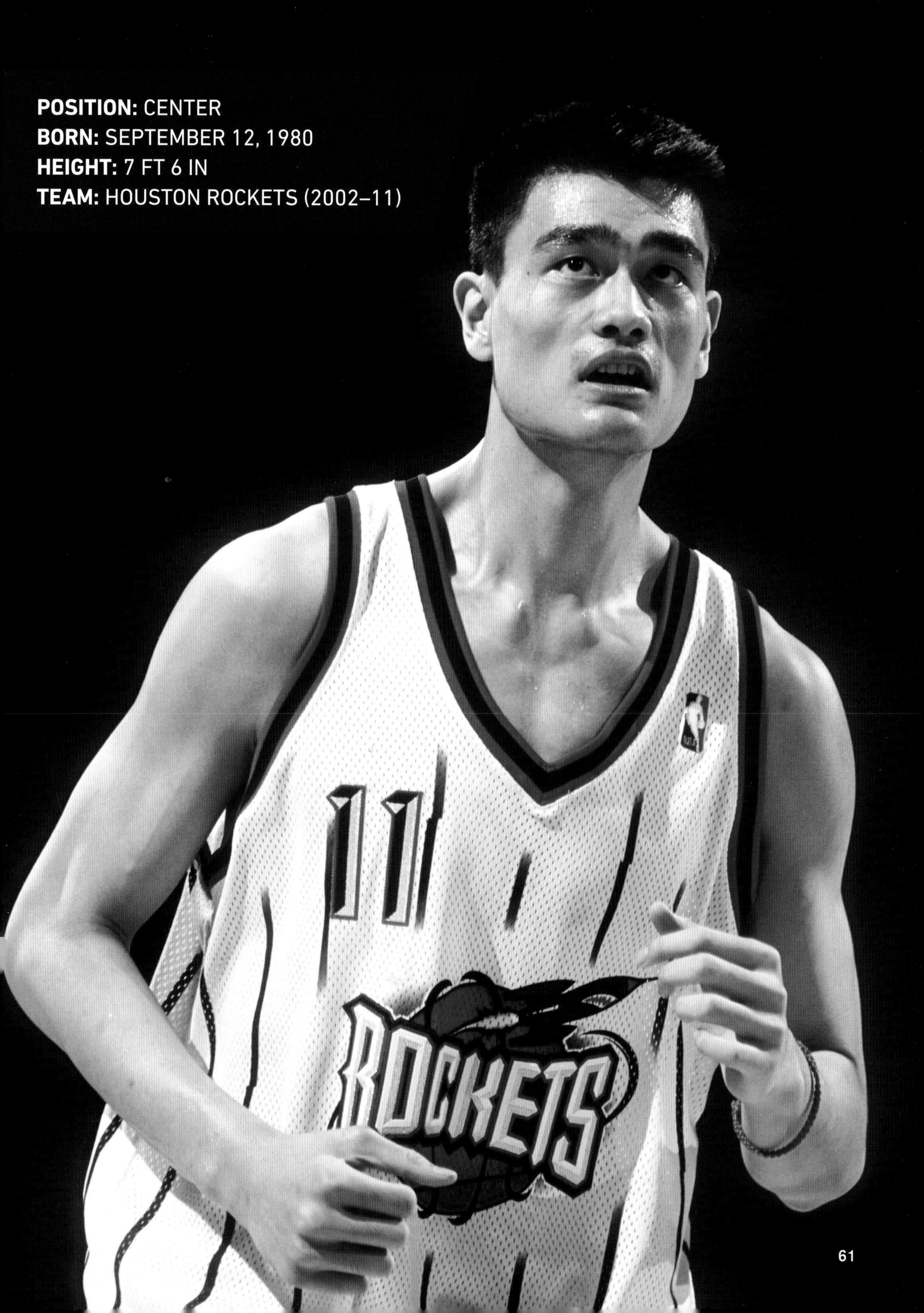

Kobe Bryant and Ronny Turiaf fight to stop Kevin Garnett from scoring in a Lakers vs. Celtics game at the 2008 NBA finals.